Longings of My Heart

TO THE GOD OF ISRAEL

ASHIRAH AZRIEAL

Library of Congress Control Number: 2021900984

HARDBACK: 978-1-954673-56-4
PAPERBACK: 978-1-954673-55-7
EBOOK: 978-1-954673-57-1

Ordering Information:

For orders and inquiries, please contact:
1-888-404-1388
www.goldtouchpress.com
book.orders@goldtouchpress.com

Printed in the United States of America

CONTENTS

PART 1
AUTOBIOGRAPHY, SCRIPTURES, AND TESTIMONIES

PART 2
WRITINGS, PSALMS, AND POEMS

PART 3
SONGS OF THE LORD

To the God of Israel

To the God of Israel, the holy one who never fails, blessed is he who formed the heavens and the earth. Who teaches my hands to war and my heart to praise. Living to make my life so free till in your image I am made.

Part 1

AUTOBIOGRAPHY, SCRIPTURES, AND TESTIMONIES

My Life in a Nutshell

Hello, my name is Chant'e Shirelle Holsey, and I am one of five siblings. My parents, Ralph and Eva Holsey, both suffered from some type of mental illness. Between my mom's multiple personalities and my dad's paranoia, normalcy was absent in our life.

One time I saw my mom hovering over my dad with a knife. The only thing I said was "O God, please don't let my mommy kill my daddy." I was about twelve. We lived in motel after motel until I reached the age of fourteen. Times of extreme abuse caused me to escape to my mind a lot. In these times of hardships, the Lord was ever with me. Throughout these ordeals, God was preparing me. My mother would sit us five down, and we would have questions and answers. We also sang to the Lord together; all this was leading up to this present day. The stories of the Israelites and the power that God displayed constantly had my mind wondering about God and Jesus. At one point, I was watching a movie called *King of Kings* and thought to myself, "Why do they have this man who looks like a surfer acting like Jesus?" Later I started having a desire to walk where Jesus walked (as a child). When I was five years old, I accepted Jesus into my heart. When I was about eleven, I started wanting to get married to a Jewish man, and I would always seek out kids who I thought looked Jewish to hang out with. Some of them were Spanish speaking. I knew nothing about Sephardic Jews at that time.

As time pressed on and I grew older like most young people, I wanted to live my own life. I loved God, but my heart was foolish.

In Later Years

In May 1994, my mother died. After her death, I started backsliding. I was always at a club somewhere with some man or woman. I had forsaken the way of truth to live in sin. I was introduced to the homosexual scene in my college years. I was taken to eighteen-and-over dance clubs, and they were all gay clubs. One night we had a function called a box social. This was done with the hopes of raising funds and a chance to get a date. The women would prepare the meal, and the guys who bought the meal would get the girl too! I prepared a steak dinner with rice and spinach. I was not picked, and some of the other girls in my group were not chosen either, so we decided to go out somewhere to ease our pain of rejection. We ended up in a place called the Arena. Eighteen and over and gay. The first thing I saw scared me—two women in the corner. I was scared! So my friends and I tried to stay close to one another. I went to the restroom, and when I thought someone was sick, I left. The next thing I knew, this short black chick was following my friends and me around the club, trying to get with me. After that night, I found myself going to clubs like that all the time. Most of my male friends were gay; I discovered I was wanted and desired for who I was and what I looked like.

My first experience was with a woman who was forty-five years old. I was in a relationship with her for about a year or so. One day we were talking, and she said out of her mouth, "I love Jesus." I thought to myself, "If you loved Jesus, you would not be with me." We were an abomination before God. So after that, she left me, and I was broken for a year. I was proposed to and about to marry someone I did not love. It would have been over in less than a year.

God's Ways Are Not Our Ways

Shortly after the proposal, we went to celebrate at the club and lo there she was. Shortly after seeing her again, I broke the engagement to be with her. During this time, God did a work in my heart and had me break up with her. I did not know at that time that God was with me, and he dismissed her through me. I just knew I had to let her go. God brought this woman back into my life to keep me from marrying and afterward healed me from my pain of losing her. You're awesome and mighty to save. This is just one of the sins of my past. There are times I would feel so alone and lonely that I would go with the first man who would give me attention.

In addition to playing a harlot with men and women, I had a smoking habit—cigarettes, cigars, beedied, cloves black, mildes, etc. I had a bad problem with masturbation. I was a complete mess until I understood the gospel. The love of God set me free.

Moreover brethren, I declare unto you the gospel which I preach unto you, which also you have received and wherein you stand by which you are also saved if you keep unto memory what I preached unto you, unless you have believed in vain for I delivered unto you first of all that which I also received how messiah died for our sins according to the scriptures and that he was buried and that he rose again the third day according to the scriptures. Connection to *Torah*: (1 Cor. 15:1–4)

The Lord thy God shall rise up unto thee a prophet, from the midst of thee, of thy brethren like unto me, unto him ye shall hearken. (Deut. 18:15)

Think not that I have come to destroy the "law," or the prophets: I am not come to destroy but to fulfill. For verily I say unto you, till heaven and earth pass away [and I think heaven and earth are still here] not one jot or tittle shall in no wise pass from the "law" until all be fulfilled whosoever therefore shall break one of these commandments, and shall teach others to do so, he shall be called the least in the kingdom of heaven: but whosoever shall do and teach them, the same shall be called great in the kingdom of heaven for I say unto you except your righteousness shall exceed the righteousness of the scribes and Pharisees, ye shall in no case enter into the kingdom of heaven. (Matt. 5:17–20)

Lift up your eyes to the heavens, and look unto the earth beneath: for the heavens shall vanish away like smoke, and the earth shall wax old like a garment, and they that dwell there in shall die in like manner: but my salvation shall be forever, and my righteousness shall not be abolished: hearken unto me, ye that know righteousness, the people in whose heart is my "law." (Isa. 51:6–7)

Imagine that you are a great designer, and you manufactured a machine that was not totally independent of you. And you give this thing all your strength and time and invest in it to make it your best creation. It is a masterpiece, and the only thing you can say is "this thing is very good." Imagine you gave it freedom to move and go where it wanted, yet your desire was for it to want you. Then one day, your creation decides that you are not a good designer nor what you have is best for it. Imagine trying to show you care for it year after year and day after day, yet it continues to behave as if it hates you. What would you do to that wicked creation?

Let's say you are a single unit, man and woman. You are *Echad* (one), and you decide to bring a child into this world. The woman would have to go through nine months of carrying this child. After this child is born, you look at it and love it. As it starts to grow, you have dreams of good things for it— to help it, to teach it to walk in wisdom and light. However, the child follows a way that leads to destruction. This child becomes an adult, is in and out of prison and drugs, and is constantly stealing from you, even physically abusing you. What would you do?

Let's say you're a faithful, godly man, and you are serving the Lord with all your strength, and your wife is not, and you find her with someone who is supposed to be your friend. What would you do?

This Is What Jesus Did

Yeshua (Jesus) came down in the form of a man through a virgin birth, was circumcised on the eighth day, was baptized in the Jordan, was led into the wilderness, was tempted by the adversary (devil) and came out victorious, healed all manner of illness, and cast out all manner of demons from death and dumb spirits to the mentally ill. He

was lied on
was set up
was betrayed
was denied
was abandoned
was captured
was jailed
was beaten
was spat on
was slapped
was scourged
was humiliated
was mocked
was given a crown of thorns
was given way more than forty lashes minus one
was placed on a stake

had spikes driven into his hands and feet
was pieced in the side and was hung naked while people continued to mock and scorn him

He did all this and more than I can ever imagine. He, being God in the flesh, allowed his own creation to murder him.

His Own Creation Murdered Him!

How many times have parents said, "I brought you into this world, I will take you out." His own creation murdered him; murder is a deliberate killing of another. And God allowed it—the love of Christ.

America, Repent

Whenever we think of people who are in need of help, we think of the little starving children in third-world countries like Africa. True, these children need help, but not as much as Americans do. The funny thing about it is when you go to Africa or Asia and preach the gospel, they get free. When we preach the gospel in America, people get bound. We need to repent.

Now I beseech you brethren, by the name of our lord Jesus Christ that you all speak the same thing, that there be no divisions among you; but that you be perfectly joined together in the same mind and the same judgment for it has been declared unto me my brethren, by them which is of the house of chio'e, that there are contentions among you now this I say, to everyone of you, say, I am of Paul; and, I am of Apollo's, and, I am of Cephas; and I am of Christ. (1 Cor. 1:10–13)

Is Christ divided? Was Paul crucified for you? Or were you baptized in the name of Paul? Does this not sound familiar? How about "we do not speak in tongues" or dance in church? I am a Baptist, I am Pentecostal, I am Lutheran. Wickedness is what this is. What about reading, studying, and rightly dividing the word of truth?

We Here in America Love Our Demons

I was talking with a coworker, and she started telling me about her trip to Las Vegas. She had so much fun, gambling and winning money, so I started telling her I found out that I had been unconsciously allowing secular music to minister to me, sitting in restaurants, etc. I went home and started praying. God released me from three unclean spirits that night. She asked me not to tell her those things. She said I was scaring her. I asked her, "Do you watch horror movies?" She said, "Sometimes." I asked her where she thought they got the idea for some of those things she watched. "I don't want to hear it," she replied. I asked her, "Why do you think when you go to a place that sells alcohol, it reads beer, wine, and spirits on the wall?" She had no reply.

I Got Liberty

This is a common statement I hear when talking to Christians. I got liberty. This is true, but we are called to be holy. The first thing people say is "we are not under that Old Testament stuff anymore. We are free; so we can eat what we want, say what we want, watch what we want, and do what we want. And "you" have no right to judge me. I hear this a lot, "You are not my judge." I don't want to tell people anything because the love that would correct them will also be rejected and ignored.

We are not supposed to have premarital relations. God is so merciful; he did make provisions for our lack of self-control. "If they cannot contain, let them marry. Marriage is good" (1 Cor. 7:9). Deut. 22: 28–29 says that if a man finds a damsel that is a "virgin," is not betrothed, lays hold of her, and lays with her; then the man who lays with her shall give unto her father fifty shekels of silver. And she shall be his wife because he has humbled her, and he may not put her away all his days. I always thought this was harsh for the woman. After having been "raped," she has to be his wife. Thank God for Jesus! Remember what happened to Ammon and Tamar in 2 Sam. 13:10–32.

Ammon wanted to lay with Tamar, so he tricked her into coming into his house with a lie of sickness. She, being obedient to her father's voice, went to him; and he forced her to have relations with him. Afterward she suggested to do things right, and he despised her. He hated her, and it was he who was wrong. This ended years later with his death. These things happen when we go out of God's order. I am not saying that all the time, marriage is first because when a man lays with a woman the two are already one. They become one in flesh and in spirit. Now, just in case you are wondering, I am single and have been for twelve years. At first, it was hard because I was still watching movies with nudity, romance, and all that stuff that is not real. Once I shut down the movies, I began to receive strength because I was not filling my heart with lust anymore. I did have one date last year; and the only reason I did that was because after nine years, you start feeling like a big reject, especially when there are three marriages in one year among the new people in your congregation.

I met this man while I was at work. He asked for my number; I gave it. This was a tough time for me. We talked on the phone for eight months, and then he asked me out—first date in four years. Of course, his plan was to lay with me. What was my heart? To be held. I prayed a lot during that time and found myself allowing him to come to my apartment alone at night, yet I prayed for God's mercy and protection. God's hand was with me, and he did not allow me to be defiled. Oh, the mercy of God! That man could have done anything, but God did not let him. Since then, I have kept my eyes on Jesus, the true lover of my soul, and he will not force himself on me. He is gentle and caring the way husbands are supposed to be, dwelling with the woman as the weaker vessel and with understanding.

I will now share a little about my first trip to Israel. As stated before, as a child of about nine years of age, I looked up to the ceiling and said I am going to go to Israel. Here is my testimony of how God answered one of my childhood prayers.

My First Trip

Last March 9, 2004, I cannot eat or sleep in anticipation of my first trip on an airplane. Yes, I finally made my first trip on a plane at the age of twenty-eight. I was terrified not for the news reports of the fighting, but for my first plane takeoff. God was with me all the way. At 3:00 a.m., we arrived in Tel Aviv, Israel, and I was beside myself. I passed the first and second check, and I was in. I went to pick up my luggage and saw a sign that read, "Welcome home, Israel agency." I nearly flipped because the first picture on the wall was a little Ethiopian girl, which is part of my heritage. I have been told that my mother's side of the family are Ethiopians.

From the time, I can remember I wanted to live like the people in the Bible; and at a young age of nine years old, I dreamt of going to the places Jesus walked. I thought… if I could just walk on the same dust that he walked on.

I was attending services in Riverside, California. During the course of this time, I felt we needed to start having meals after services. People were invited over and I would cook for them, and we would have a blessed time. All was well until my sister and I were forced to move from this house, and after we moved, others had tried to continue in this. But I stopped attending. They were having alcohol, secular music, and movies. The time of fellowship turned into a time of secular get-together, and again I found myself alone and trying to be around holiness.

I found myself leaving such a secular gathering, going to the Harvest Christian Bookstore, and starting to listen to some *Messianic Praise and Worship* CDs. I had been to that section before and was trying to find one song that just would not get out of my head. All I could remember of the songs were the words "Holy, Lord, you are holy. Righteous and pure, gracious, forever faithful Lord, you are worthy forever true." Those words haunted me day and night. I had to find it. Meanwhile I was approached by a man named Daniel whom I had met two years prior to that night. He invited me to a *Simcha Torah* celebration that next Saturday.

I went and there was a six-hundred-year-old *Torah* scroll that the people were dancing with, a Rabbi, and lots of long beards. After the women were dancing a while, I prostrated myself as if I were always raised in synagogues, said the Rabbi. I soon understood the meals I was trying to do in the church service as an *oneg*. The word *oneg* means delight. We are to delight in each other as God delights in Yeshua, and Yeshua delights in us.

I soon started attending this synagogue and was introduced to Hebrew. I attended this place for a while, and during my duration there, I developed some contacts with a certain messianic congregation called Kehilat HaCarmel in the land of Israel. I found out about their intercessors call to prayer on the mountain and wanted to go.

After some time of being involved in the synagogue, I found out I was going to have issues everywhere, and this place was no different. Some of the people there thought I was trying to Christianize them, and some of the people of the church thought I was trying to make them Jewish and "put them under the law." I found myself often looking on the Internet for a combination of the two. I did not know at the time that I was looking for what apostle Paul describes in Eph. 2:15. As a new man, I just knew I needed both, and I needed to worship on Shabbats (Saturdays).

During this time of conflict, I found myself speaking to people about me going to Israel, and neither the church nor the synagogue believed I was going to go because I was a poor single black woman who could barely maintain a place to live. The people at the church thought I put myself under the law, and since I was kicked out, I was neither obeying God nor was I hearing God. I was crazy and I "left God by choosing the Jewish congregation where those Jews don't believe in Jesus" instead of that church.

One night, I was at work, and I was listening to a CD music called *Sar Shalom*. And I was really just blessed by the peace I was in. I decided to call one of my brothers and found out my phone bill was $72.18. I then said, "If you want me to go to Israel, you have to pay this phone bill and bring me finances to go." Well, I went home that night and found three checks in the mailbox adding up to $500.00. After I found the money in the mailbox, I remembered what God said to me. He said he was going to pay the bills. I was going to get a phone call from Israel and that I was going. I received a phone call at 5:17 a.m. that following Wednesday. Soon after that, the Lord began to speak to me about the trip.

A few weeks had passed now, and I was preparing to try to pay for the plane ticket that at that time was $1,256.67. We would receive e-mails on what to do, and one day after work, I was looking at the e-mails and found out that the prayers worked. And the Lord made a way, and the tickets went from $1,256.67 to $771.50. I was so happy. The next day was *Shabbat*. And after the service, a friend came to me and said he had been praying, and God told him to give me some money for my trip. I didn't ask for it; it was freely given, another $500.00. God is awesome and all his doings too. All these things the Lord did for me the first time I stepped out on faith and went to Israel and when everyone around me thought I was mad and I was not going.

My arrival was even better, and the duration is worth a million words so I will try only a few. From Tel Aviv to Haifa and to Jerusalem, it was a journey of a lifetime. Three times a day of prayer, praise and worship, and anointed teaching. Oh, it was wonderful. The SOM was hosted by Kehilat HaCarmel where Jews, Arabs, Russians, and now Ethiopians—as well as people from all around the world—worship the God of Israel in spirit and truth.

In Jerusalem, we went to the Western Wall. I was knocked off my feet to the ground, and a fire started bubbling in my stomach, and a language I never heard came out of my belly through my mouth.

We went to the Dead Sea and passed by what some believed to be the place where Sodom and Gomorrah once stood.

We went to Yad V'shem where the holocaust memorial is. And soon my time was coming to a close. I started thinking how I could accidentally get left behind (it did not work), and finally I was on the last plane home. In a nutshell, this was my first trip to Israel.

Linda, Bee, and myself, Chant'e, on top of the church roof overlooking Jerusalem.

It is now July 2008, and I attend a place called Beth Shalom where all people worship the living God in a first-century way. We have prayer, dancing, live worship, and teachings. It is sometimes difficult, but I know God wants unity between the two groups like what the prophet Zachariah said, "Not by power, not by might, but by your spirit says the Lord."

I don't know what God has in store for me in the upcoming years, but I will go where he wants me to go because I love him!

A Short Testimony

From sickness to health, from death to life, the Lord has done wonderful things for me. I was bound by perversion, cigarettes, and self-pity. I was also bound by self-hate, but the Lord in his mercy revealed himself to me and set me free from many demons and many strongholds. His loving kindness and tender mercy delivered me.

One such deliverance occurred while I was attending a church that, at that time, was preaching Jesus Christ and him being crucified. This message of the gospel brought power into my life.

It was Sunday afternoon, and I borrowed $5 from the pastor. I said it was for the purpose of bus fare, but it was to buy cigarettes. Well, I lost the $5; and that next Monday, after returning from work, I became quite irritated at everything and started cussing up a storm. I was so angry I smoked every cigarette that was in the house, and I went to sleep for the rest of that day.

That night, something happened to me that was as a scene out of the gospels themselves.

This night I woke up around 2:00 a.m. and started screaming. Next, I started shaking violently and I was scared, and suddenly one of my brothers told me to start praising God, so I did. As this was happening to me, the shaking became more violent. I then felt something like a ball rolling in my stomach, and the words "FLEE FROM ME SATAN" came out of my mouth. At this moment, I felt as if something was ripping out of me.

This took place shortly after I repented from my actions. I had a moment to think and realized I was not behaving in a godly manner, and I asked God to forgive me, and he did by setting me free from my bondage. Anytime something controls your attitude, you are bound by it. Thank God for Isa. 61:1–4 being fulfilled.

This is just one of the many deliverances the Lord has brought me through. He is able to go exceedingly and abundantly above all we can ask or think.

Put your trust in the lord.

Part 2

WRITINGS, PSALMS, AND POEMS

A Clean Heart

O Lord, give me a clean heart and renew a right spirit within me. You are my strength who subdues the people under me. You are the captain of my army!

Jesus, you have been my source of strength. Azriela, you have called me by name; you are my strength. My song shall I sing to you. As you have defeated the enemies of Israel, so shall you cause all who hate me to submit under me.

Come, My Beloved (Bridegroom)

My beloved, you are to me the one who restores my soul. After a long week of work, I take delight in you. You are my eternal refuge. Let the lifting of my hands be to you as the morning sacrifice and the singing of my voice a pleasing aroma. Let my dance go before you as a weave offering before your throne. You give rest to all who take delight in you. You are like a bridegroom from whom I find my strength. May the joining of our hearts together be like a wedding banquet and the unity of your people a sweet fragrance in your garden of spices.

Don't Take Your Presence from Me

God, how can I live without you? You are my father. O Lord, my strength and protection. Please don't take your presence away from me. All else is nothing before you. You shall provide all my needs according to your riches and glory. To you the earth belongs and the fullness of. Nothing compares to the promise you give to those who fear your name. I thank you, Lord, for your spirit that transforms me. Make me a woman after your own heart and cause me to know your ways. One angel calls out, and the others respond, "Kadosh, Kadosh, Kadosh Adonai, Tz va'ot."

Draw Me Near

O Lord, your words are true. You draw near those who draw near to you. Your secrets you unfold to those who know your covenant. You are a faithful God and king, those who know you understand your covenant. You are a covenant-keeping God! You are a wonderful husband, those who know you will remain faithful too. Lord, I love the way you cause my heart to leap in my chest. My God, I love you. All my flesh cries out for you! You make my bones boil within, just like lava, fire in my bones. Lord, I thank you that you have chosen the scum of the earth like myself to show your covenant to. I thank you for the privilege of serving you. You are awesome, God, God of Israel. You are holy and holy. I praise you every day forever!

God Is Love

Have you tasted love? Do you know he is good? God is love! God is good! Come and taste the Lord and know he is good. Drink from the fountain of living waters and quench your thirsty souls. Let him satisfy you right early.

Oh, in the secret place of the Almighty I will enter alone. Oh, love the Lord all you peoples. All nations shall come and see the Lord in his glory. You shall fall down before him and worship for he is great (and greatly to be praised). O Lord, you are my everything. Words are lame and cannot explain who you are.

Everyone must know you for themselves.

To the One I Love

This is for the one I love whose source of love comes from above. Only in him is this love so true—that is, this kind of love reaching from me to you.

A love so pure and deep that when I think of it I start to weep. To know someone so in the heart is better than all friendships showing in outward parts. Spiritual connection speaks ever so clear, more than ten thousand words spoken closely in the ear. To please you is a joy, and to serve you is delight. Yet this I must do to grow up to new heights—to walk in power and might, to heal the sick and raise the dead, and to shed light. My soul yearns for you, strange but true. Why is this? I haven't got a clue. Maybe it will continue to remain until the Messiah comes again and reigns. Maybe it will end in pain (may it never be).

For there is a love directed to you from me. May the love of Yeshua cover you for his love in me is strong from me to you. May his eternal burning affection fill your soul with love and delight untold. For he is love and has filled me with this love for you from above.

Simple Prayer

May you come soon, Lord. May you come soon. For there are two things I have longed for: to walk with you all the days of my life and to see your beauty.

Lord, let your glory fill this temple. Saturate my soul with your love. Make me know your still-small voice in the morning and your breath upon my neck in the evening. Oh, to know you is my heart's desire—to know you, to set my heart more on fire, to love and adore you in every way even if it shall cost me my life.

You, Lord, are the reason I live and the reason love is real. Lord, give me a clean heart that I may serve you without fear. Make my path clear so your voice alone I will hear.

Lord, thank you for this Shabbat. Shabbat is a time of receiving. Thank you, Lord, for your spirit. I need you every day.

Will you breathe on me in the midnight hours and make my heart take off in flight?

Why? Why? Why? A Million Times Why?

Lord, my Lord, why do I go about thinking what to do? Lord, my God, all I want is to worship you. Lord, my God, why are there so many issues distracting me? Lord God, why do the wicked try to oppress me? Lord, why can't I be as you have called me?

Lord, why is the world we live in so crazy? Lord, why do people try to play you?

Why do people do what they do? Why is the meaning of marriage changing?

Why are the courts making laws that offend you? Why are people so complacent about this issue?

Why can underage girls murder their unborn babies? Why are they allowed to abort an unborn child but are not allowed to receive an aspirin for cramps from the school nurse? Why is whoring allowed but the voice of abstinence forbidden?

Why do we allow young men and women to sign up to fight for this country, but they are forbidden to have a beer at eighteen. (I am not for drunkards either; but if they are old enough to die, have sex without parents' permission, and murder their unborn in secret, why not be able to drink also? All these things can cause death to more than just the individual.)

Why do we vote for a president who refuses to fight for this country when he is the commander and chief of the military?

Why? Why? Why?

I don't understand. There is a difference between a woman and a man.

Today is the day of why? Why is on my mind.

Freedom?

What is freedom, and who determines what it is? Is it the right to speak as you wish?

Is it the right to eat what you want? What is it, and where does it come from?

Does freedom give you the right to put others down? Is it okay to exalt yourself to the highest position?

Or is it to take the best places where you have been invited as a guest? Is not freedom in the ability to live without fear of violence against you?

Is it not to be able to live without being enslaved by another people group against your will? Is not freedom in the fact we can worship the one true living God without government harassment?

Desirous

More than ever, I desire your presence. To lie in my room dark and still, hearing nothing but my heart pounding because of your love.

I am lovesick; without you, I cannot see. You are my daily breath! You, Lord, are my king and I miss you.

Will you not come to me again? I long for you. In the secret place of your chambers, I stand by the door, knocking and pounding. Lord, it is I, your beloved.

There is nothing I want more than you. Lord, have your way in me. I will not deny you for I surrender to your plan. You are the potter and I the clay. Shape me for your will.

What to Say

What to say today, a good day. And I raise my hands and lift my head to pray, coming boldly to your throne of grace, knowing you are the only way.

I sit in the dark corner alone, trying to make your presence my home.

Leaning on your everlasting arm, watching and waiting for that final alarm.

Can it be that you love me, or that I am blind and cannot see?

Why do I go about seeking your approval when all is good because the sacrificed, removal. I am happy to be in your fold and where I can learn mysteries untold.

Lord, you are my one true friend, and I know on you I can trust to the end.

From the Heart

The Lord is gracious, merciful, and true. His blood has made all things new.

A tree so long ago now rose again for us to know. Sitting on the throne of righteousness for in him we take our rest. Coming soon on a cloud, out of heaven come a boom loud. He will have flames of fire in his eyes, and to some who perish, he will come as a surprise.

So now I stand and wait for he it is I anticipate, to bring me rest from my work and to rid me of this place I lark. Wanting and waiting to be gone for the full redemption of my soul that, I long.

A walk in a body so new, free from sin and sickness too!

My heart's cry as a child was to be like Enoch and be taken out.

So now I remember it as clear as day, longing for my life to end that way.

Looking for my Messiah is truly my heart's one desire!

Love with someone might be fun, but he can never be the only one. My life is to please the Lord. Truly he is all I am living for.

Authority

All power and all authority have been given to me. Go ye therefore.

Today is a new day, and the glory of God is from everlasting to everlasting. I just thought I'd write a little about authority this morning. Yeshua is the final authority on earth and has given all his followers his authority. So if you want to walk in the manifest power of God Most High, believe in his words spoken in Mark chapter 16: 16–19, and it is good to read the whole book of Mark if not just the whole chapter.

During this time of seeking the Lord, I was reminded of this fact. He is able to do exceedingly and abundantly all we can ask or think according to the power that works in us. Without mention of age, group, or sex (M or F), mentioning it is accessible to all believers. May the Lord raise up those who are down and bring to maturity those who are lacking in the power of God.

From Me to You

My heart cries out, cries out to you! My thoughts think only, only of you.

For you are my sword and shield. All my delight is in you. How can this be a love so free from me to you and from you to me? How tender is your touch. It is like a summer's breeze. For you are my song! In the rain, you bring the brightness of the sun through all the pain. I love you for this love is true. It is only from you to me and me to you.

Open Romance with the King of Kings, Yeshua (a.k.a. Jesus)

Your taste is sweet like honey. Your breath within makes my heart skip a beat, my love, my fair one, my relief. You are God Most High. You are my everything, my every day. You are my constant desire in every way. To sit under the shadow of your wings gives meaning to my life. O Lord, thank you for romancing me. I will share this love open and free.

Deeper and Deeper with You

Not very much to say, but my one desire is to go deeper, so deep. I want to feel your spirit deep in my soul. I want your radiance to overcome me. Let my life be like a rose in a thorn bush and let my lips satisfy you early. Let the raising of my hands bring you pleasure, O Lord. I shall not be ashamed of this love that is true for you said, "If you are ashamed of me, I will be ashamed of you. If you confess me, I will confess you before my father in heaven." Let my openness bring you glory and draw others deeper in you.

Openly

Love today is hard to find. Love today has had one thing in mind. Love today in the world is a lie for true love was crucified.

He hung on a tree for you and for me, was mocked and scorned, and treated shamefully. To him I owe my life, the one who paid the bride-price.

To give him all of me not in the dark but openly for all to see. Oh yes, for all to see.

He was naked on a tree for me, so I shall expose my heart's condition open for him. It's the least I can do. He has done it all for me on a hill in a place called Calvary.

Maybe

Good morning, Lord! How are you? It is I again calling, crying to you. Maybe if I were married, it would not be so; but until that time comes, I'll never know. Maybe if I had not gone astray after my mother went to her grave. Maybe if I had a daughter, my life would revolve around her. But wait, who would be her father? Maybe if I were an officer or lawyer, I could throw myself in my work, but then my mind might go berserk. Dealing with others' pain all day would cause anyone to go insane. What should I do with my time? sit and wonder "what ifs" all day in my mind? To know you more is what I live for, to do those things not done before.

Greater works than these are what you said, maybe even raise someone from the dead. So let these hands press on ahead.

Maybe someone needs to know you in an intimate way but does not have the words to say. So maybe, if I write my heart, someone might get a jump start.

Lord, let these words be true; and maybe in your courts, I can recite them to you! Blessed be the name of the Lord forever.

O

O God, you have opened my heart to your love, and it is so good. Like the morning dew or a spring sky, the Lord's love runs deep. Into your eyes I gaze as you make my heart pound with uncontrolled excitement. Yes, to wait under the shadow of your wings. I cannot think of what to say; I only know what I feel.

How can this be? Lord, let the light of your continence shine on me till you are fully exalted. Be lifted up in my life, and let your spirit reign in me!

Love Affair

Let him kiss me with his kisses so tender and sweet for to him and him alone do I find release. From the cares of the world and all the pain, and only through him will come rivers of rain. Clouds full of water end the drought and bring forth oceans to swim about—not to the ankles or to the knees, but to swim in them if you please. This love affair I have is too divine and, with man, would be hard to find. Yet the image of God is male and female for in Genesis, this was a foretelling of what was to come. Two joined in marriage would become one.

Lord, you are my love and my only one. I would love to marry and have his left hand under my head and his right arm embracing me whoever he is. But until that is a reality, your love is all I need.

Rain Down

Rain down, Lord, on me. Send your living waters. My heart cries out and even thirsts for you. Give me a drink so I can be satisfied. O Lord, you are worthy of all praise, and you are my eternal desire. All else is nothing before you, and nothing compares to you. Worthy are you, Lord, from the highest heaven to the lowest valley. Your name is to be praised. Give me the ability.

Expectant Desperation

The Lord is on my side; how can man disturb me? I wait all day long for his judgments to come and overtake me. He is like a ship ready to dock, dropping off precious cargo. His *ruach* is much sought after, and his presence is amazing. He is the righteous king who renders justice to the oppressed. You, Lord, are my only desire, truly you are. I long to gaze into your fire. You are a fire.

You came to me, and I was unafraid for your throne was illuminated with sparks of flames, and as your throne came closer to me, I could only scream "OH YEAH, YEAH." How glorious is your fire. After you left me, I could not speak for a short time. For the kindling of a fire in my belly and brightness of the light, all I could do was sit and hold myself tight.

Let that fire rekindle in my belly again.

The Lord Is

The Lord is like water refreshing the soul. The Lord is like chocolate, sweet to the taste. The Lord is like a wallet full of money; you'll never want to lose it.

The word of the Lord is like food, needed every day. The word of the Lord is like a rock. You can rest on it.

The word of the Lord is like fire, purifying the heart.

The name of the Lord is a strong tower. The name of the Lord is sweet like honey.

The name of the Lord is like oil dripping, dripping. Oh, the name of the Lord is so good.

Come, taste and see that the Lord is gracious to those who seek him, who seek him in truth. Come and bow down at his throne.

Repentance

The act of repentance is very sweet. The love of God will give us a needed release. So pure and holy is his name. To blaspheme it would be a shame. So call upon him in times of distress for only in him will you find sure rest. The Lord is good in all he does. Love him for nothing, just because. He did however love you first; therefore go to him to quench your thirst. Live life as if there is no tomorrow so that each day you will lack sorrow. Open your eyes to see the light and worship the Lord all your might.

I Will

I will sing unto the Lord a new song. In the morning, he shall hear my voice.

I will open my mouth and make his name glorious. He is Jesus, the holy and awesome one. I will not be ashamed of my past for he has done a good work in me. He has done these things so that I may witness his great forgiveness and mercy. Therefore I will sing to him, and I will proclaim his name. Only he is holy. No one else will ever get his glory in my life. I will make your name glorious, Yeshua, Adonai.

With Love,
Azriela Bat Sarah

Just a Poem

Lord, I will worship you with all of me. I will worship you for your love has set me free.

I will sing to you all day long. I will sing to you my song. Love is wonderful in every way. In your presence, I long to stay. You are the one who makes me know love. And only true love comes from you. You are God, and in to your courts, I will stay each and every day.

The Lord Is My Light

Who is a light like the light of lights? He is the lesser light by night and the great light by day. He is a pure and perfect way. He is my God, and there is none other.

Who is a god like the God of Israel? No one. I will worship him for he is marvelous and worthy.

Truth in the Inward Part

I am thankful that I can be truthful with the Lord concerning everything. I just want to say sometimes the truth hurts, but it is for our own good. I will not walk in a lie to anyone. I am not going to fake it till I make it. I will walk in light, and the Lord will do the rest. There is no good thing in man. We are not able to do good outside of him, and I am going to seek his face, and he will answer me. He will release me and set me free, and I will be a witness unto him in truth. Father, I am asking you to help me so that I can shine as I once did.

Lord, let me shine for you once again.

Sincerely,
Ashirah Azriela

The Lord Is My Strength

Lord, you are the source of my strength, and I need you every day. My heart longs for you in a land full of terror. The people have set themselves against me for observing your laws. Lord, your words are pure and peaceable. Your words change the soul from the inside out. You are holy, and holy ones praise you every day forever.

What Is Love?

Love is a strange thing. Sometimes heartache and pain it brings, ripping and tarring the soul. How can love make one whole? Love makes the strong weak. Love is often mistaken, never thought of as meek.

Love makes one overlook, and that is why mercy is mistook.

Love is willingly blind, wanting to forgive and willing to be kind. Love brings pain often giving yet having nothing to gain.

Love is free yet costing everything even in times of sadness.

Love makes your heart sing. True love comes with many woes, but for those who never loved, it is something you'll never know.

Love is patient, long-suffering, and true. And I know I have found this love in YOU.

Lord, you are the reason I live. To you, my heart and soul I give. You are my Lord. Your name is Yeshua, and you are my Lord.

Husband and children I have none, but all is well and good as long as we are one.

You are God alone, and I worship you. Help me be all you want for me.

For it is for you, I do what I do.

A New Song

Sing unto the Lord a new song and tell of his marvelous works. He has torn the veil that separated me from him. He is my life and the length of my days. For him is my soul crying out all day. To sit in his shadow comforts me. To be in his presence is what I need; it sets me free more and more. I will praise your name; the more I praise you, the less I am ashamed. You are love; all I ever wanted was in you. I can heal the sick, do signs and wonders, and speak in tongues—even raise the dead. But knowing you is all I want instead. Loving you is what I live for. You it is I adore.

Thirsty 1

Lord God, my time is in your hands, and my heart pants for you like a deer after water. My soul is empty without you. I have no time alone with you. I awake too late, and I am constantly interrupted while trying to worship you. I am too tired to stay up late at night, and when I do, I get called. Lord, when will I be able to have time alone with you? My dad's always bugging, and the phone ringing, and the supervisors calling. My life is a mess. Lord, I long to spend my days in your word and my nights in your presence. Lord, fill me once again with your fire for it is what keeps me refreshed.

Thirsty 2

For his is the kingdom and power. He is the king. I long to sit under the shadow of his wings to gaze in his eyes so true. To seek him alone, this I want to do.

He is the love of my life; even in times of pain and distance, his voice suffices. I want to feel his passion so near and the sweet sound of his heartbeat to draw me near. To call on his name when I feel so far away often brings a spark, so with all of me, I will worship him even with all my heart. I never could have found a love so true if I started slipping away from you. Lord, you are my focus from this day on and this life anew as though reborn. How can I show my love for you? Lord, I know you know already, but I like to express it to you. Ten thousand songs are in my heart, but my actions will show what is in the inward parts. Have a wonderful evening, Lord, and I will rise up early to adore you. You're so beautiful in all you do. All I want is to express my love for you.

Prayer

O Abba, you know my going and coming and my rising and falling. I seek you for only you know what I am going through. I am totally ready to follow you to my death, but it's the leaving behind I will regret. "Come and follow me" is what you have said. To live as a sacrifice, I'm no good if I'm dead. You are truly my one desire, but my soul has now finally understood desire, something I never knew till I settled to the place I call home. You and only you know the pain I feel. Never knowing these types of emotions were true. I pray that you would bless those I love with an incredible feeling of my love for I love them with love so true that it only could come from you. A love so pure and deep is the kind of love that makes me weep. To walk in this is more than bliss, and it will be something I will really miss. Maybe it does not have to be that way; maybe it will always stay. I hope it does for now and ever, and I hope we part never. Let our bond stay for all eternity because this bond is what I need.

So, Lord, I pray you hear me today and cause your favor to fall on me, for all my life is before you, and let me serve you eternally.

Preoccupied

Preoccupied. What shall I do? My soul longs for you. My heart is being tossed to and fro. So I don't want to feel anymore a mission for one and a duty for the other. Why, when we're all sisters and brothers? One new man is what it's about. So why do I have to yell and shout, defending my home no matter the wrong? O Lord, I wonder how long. A good friend is so hard to find. Yet love makes one blind. How can I live this way, hoping and praying for unity? This day, one Christian loves the truth yet with misunderstanding of the Jews. A covenant home where love was not cheap is a high price I paid, and here comes the thief. He comes to steal, kill, and destroy. But it made me hold on the more. Now I feel slow, pulling at my heart. All I wanted was prayer, not a new start. The Lord will be my judge and savior. I wish I could have signed a waiver. I am stuck in the middle of a battle. And just like a cowgirl, my horse I will saddle, ready for the ride about to take place and looking forward to finishing this race. My hope is in you, Lord, and I need you to guide me all the way so that you will be glorified this day. Teach me your ways and all you do so that my character will always reflect you. I don't want to quench your spirit, yet getting it from multiple directions is too much for me to bear. Lord, give me your words to share. Help me walk in light so that I will take wings and flight.

And He Walks with Me

Looking forward to the prize ahead. Glad to be among the living and not dead. Waiting to enter eternal life and be that perfect bride. You were willing to go to the grave, so in pain, a roadway I will pave. So what else is there to do but offer my life as a living sacrifice to you? How will I praise you from the earth? Who will exult you if I am gone? Will the dust praise you? Okay, maybe the rocks will cry out, but why is that necessary when you have human beings with free will and a mouth to proclaim your goodness? With all that is in me, I will praise you. Let my life speak louder than my words. Let the voice of singing please you in the morning and the sacrifice of praise for a broken heart move you at night. What a life to live, never a dull moment.

Rivers of Pleasure

As I open my mouth and let out a cry, tears roll down my cheeks from my eyes, wanting, praying, and hoping for more. Your presence, Lord, is what I hunger and thirst for—to swim in the ocean so deep and wide that hours on in I will still abide. Oh, you are truly good, and holiness is so misunderstood. To be one with you is a wonderful thing. Open my heart to feelings unknown.

What else is there to say, just that I love you, Lord, love you in every way.

Take not your Holy Spirit from me.

Power

Now is the time to walk in faith—giving up myself, not trying to be great, letting the hope of fame die down so the power of God may fully abound.

My passion in life is to do his will, but first I must learn to sit and be still. Soon and soon, he will arise; and healing, deliverances, signs, and wonders will be done before my eyes. So I sing hallelujah today, and on my face, I will pray to experience his glory in a more powerful way for his mighty hand leads the way.

Under his canopy, I will stay until he comes for me one day.

When My Enemies Fall

When my enemies rise, they will fall. They who hate me will draw back suddenly and unaware. They will draw back and repent from their evil intentions. I will bless the Lord who upholds me for he is my resting place. I called upon the Lord in times of trouble, and he has sustained me.

It's All Good

The Lord is my life and strength; he is my victory. As liars go before his throne, accusing and pointing fingers, he is my defense. Just as Job was accused before the father, so was I. I have only been sent as a blessing; my will to live is to serve. I have a desire for marriage if it is your will, O God. I love you more than life. I will be pleased only to awaken in your likeness. May you send the Holy Spirit to me quickly that I may fulfill my duty than take me home. For this life is not worth what I could have with you.

A Dream, A Vision

A dream, a vision. So real, so real. I was there seen and can feel. I heard the sounds and observed the signs around, and darkness was like the midnight sky. There were dead carcasses, meek and wild dinosaurs, a horse, a dog, and a lion so brave. There were also two men. The thing I saw was something strange, but I believe that it was arranged. I saw one of the men casting a net with meat at the end and the dog gorging the lion. The lion was lying down bleeding, trying to defend itself. The dog was on top of a log and was ripping the lion to pieces. The horse was supposed to help the lion but was distracted, running after the meat. The man was holding a fishing pole. I went to him, but he hadn't gotten it yet. I wanted to help the lion, but I knew it was not my battle, so I then crossed over to the light and told the man to get his shoe. I was still trying to help the lion. I was angry at the men, and the horse was stupid. I woke up and wrote it down; maybe the Lord will show me what this means. I have a thought; but, Lord, it may not be true. So I will leave the interpretations up to you.

The Interpretation

The two men are two masters. The horse and the state we are in are wavering to and fro between two masters, and the fishing pole and line are our fleshly desires distracting us. The lion is Jesus (Yeshua) who is like a lamb, silent before the dog gorging him. But every time the dog tries to leave the log, he, the lion, stands on hind legs, stops him from moving, then would lie down, and take abuse of the dog as long as he is not trying to move from the log.

I have never been the one who was dream-oriented, but this scared me. And I have been seeking God all day about this as well as people to confirm interpretations. Be not conformed to this world but be transformed by the renewing of your mind. Put on Christ, and be not tossed by every wind and doctrine, but that which is sound. Yeshua was crucified and, more so, has risen from the dead so that we may walk in power.

A Time

The Lord's time of deliverance is near, a time that comes every year. A time of reflections of the Lord's sacrifice, a time to realize we don't own our own lives. A time to see the coming king. A time to know our freedom ring. Only in the Lord of host is there room for anyone to boast. May HaShem bless his name this year, and may a sign of his coming appear. May the God of glory give us peace, and exchange stress for release—an incredible release.

More Power, More Pressure

We must fight to the end; we must not quit. The more we overcome, the more we win. HaSatan and his angel are working hard by night to bring terror upon me and put me to flight. But the Lord is my shepherd and my strong tower so that I may stand in the darkest hour. I press on the mark of the high call to give up my life, not some but all. I must take up the cross daily.

To him alone belongs glory and truth, to him alone. Lord, in these coming days, let your spirit take over my way and spread over me your shelter.

To Live Is Messiah, to Die Is Gain

The Lord is my strength and shield; for him my soul long. A day in his courts is better than a thousand days anywhere else. The more my heart yearns for companionship, the more I realize only he can satisfy my needs. He is the lover of my soul, and for him my body quivers.

Oh, the more I desire love and closeness, the more I want to be in his presence. Holy is the Lord and worthy to be praised. I love you, Lord. You are my life and the length of my days. For you and in you alone I live.

What Power

Oh, you are powerful, God. You are mighty. There is none besides you. You inhabit all creation. O Lord, the power you possess is unsearchable. You, Lord, are the source of all power. Jesus, demons tremble at your word, and the weak call on your name for you are our strong champion. O Lord, you made all things; the worlds were formed through your word. O Jesus, you made all things for your pleasure. You are glorious. Have your way in me. I am your handmaid, and you are my master. Lead me in paths that bring me to you. O Lord, I could kiss you. You are forever my eternal delight. I will always worship you for you are worthy. The angels bow before you and adore you saying, "Kadosh, Kadosh, Kadosh Adonai, Tz va'ot" (Holy, holy, holy is the Lord, God of Armies). You are the commander in chief. Powerful are you, Lord, mighty in all your ways.

When the Enemy Rises against Me

Lord, how has the enemy raised his tongue against me? With lying words and bitter hatred, they slander me. It is you whom I trust. I will call out to my God, and he will save me from my enemy who puffs at me. My God is king over the universe, and he is the one who controls the roaring of the seas. Lord, look down upon the wicked who persecute my soul for your name's sake and who, with lying tongues, try to bring my head to the dust. Yet I will still praise you for you have said that they called the master prince of demons. What will they do to the students?

If they will hate the Lord, they will hate me too. I will always bless the Lord for he has done wonderful things. And I will always praise him for he is my defense, and I shall not be moved.

Therefore my heart rejoices, and my glory shall sing praises to you.

Forever, Lord, I will love you.

Who Is This King Who Stole My Heart?

Who is this king I cannot see yet I know? Who is he who has won my soul?

Who is the Lord of Glory I have not seen, yet I have been to the secret place with?

How I love to be called to the chamber of the bridegroom, to behold his glory, to prostrate before him, to behold him face-to-face.

Who is this king who has captured my heart? whose presence is my constant desire? It is my constant meditation, my eternal desire, oh yeah, my eternal flame!

I love you, Lord. All my springs are in you!

Why Do People Rage

Lord, how have the enemies increased who hate you? All day long, they go about seeking to upset those quiet in the land. They seek to cause the just to slip by rebellion. Lord, give me the strength to not wish harm on those who willingly try to cause me to show unsound emotions of anger and frustration. Lord, even if you allowed it, I will not allow the enemy to outwit me. I will hold my peace until you have seen me to be faithful and unmoved in trusting you even when you allow things to try to rob my peace. Let me not wish harm of the foolish, but let me remember I once was foolish as well. Lord, I thank you for your mercy on my life for without it, I might have done something harmful to someone by now. You are ever merciful on the children of men. Help me, I pray. Be as dust before the wind to those who anger me.

The One Who Is to Be Feared

O Lord, you are holy; holy ones praise you every day forever! As the angels stand before your throne, so will I always worship you. You are holy, and your name is holy!

I will bow down to the one who has captured my heart and the one in whom is all delight—Yeshua, Jesus, the lover of my soul. Bow down all the earth before him and render praise. Surrender to his will. Jesus, you make my heart skip! To rest in your presence is my only desire. Let the fire of your love pierce my soul and transform me.

The Resurrection

God is so gentle and sweet. To see him in his glory is sweet. He has restored that which was lost. The Lord is great in all the earth; his works speak of his wonder. He is God; without him nothing exists. He made all things for his glory. All things. Satan is also a creation of the Creator. He can do nothing without permission of God. Job was righteous, and none was like him when the sons of God went before the throne of God; so was HaSatan. He accused Job before God (he is the accuser of the brethren), and God gave him leave but told him not to take his life. Nothing exists outside of God. He is the creator of everything. Jesus, for him and by him were all things created. You are awesome, God! Oh, praise the Lord, all ye people and worship at his footstool for he alone is worthy.

Love the Lord with all your heart and give him all your strength, and he shall restore your soul.

This Love Affair with Jesus

Your taste is sweet to my lips. As chocolate melts within my mouth, your love melts me to buttery liquid. Lord, you make my heart leap for you.

All my body shakes with desire to feel your presence around me.

Jesus, you are my love and the one in whom all is my delight (you are the one my heart beats for). Each day, I long only to feel your presence around me, to hear your voice. O Lord, your voice is as soothing as a melody playing in my heart; your presence is as sweet as the aroma around me, as sweet as cinnamon; and you are a delightful fragrance. When I am with you, no one else exists. You are my all and all.

Never leave me and never let me go with your love surrounding me and your tender mercies abounding.

Thank you for drawing me near and showing me what love is.

To Know You More

To know you more is my pure delight, to gaze into your eyes so beautiful and bright, to eat at your table with all pleasant fruit, and to bathe in the essence that is purely you. All my heart cries day in and day out to the one who turns my life about, to show forth his glory and his praise, to proclaim the name of Jesus (Yeshua) all my days. Jesus, savior, the one I adore—my life, my source, and the one my heart beats for. Loving Father and gentle healer, when you call, I will answer.

Why I Was Created

To worship you, Lord, is better than life itself. To stand in your presence is all that I desire. O Lord, to be separated from you is like death itself; not being able to ascribe greatness to your name is like a day without sunlight. I long to praise you (in the assembly of the upright). As a wife waits for the return of her husband, so my heart eagerly waits for my time in the secret place with you. Oh, I will utter your praises, Lord, all day long for you are mine and I am yours.

Jesus, I seek you in the day; and at night, I am not silent. Holy and just are you in all your ways. Your works are glorious from the beginning till now. Lord, you make me sing in the morning.

You Are

Lord, you are evermore pleasing than all pleasant foods. You are more glorious than a king's palace, and you have more radiance than a queen. Lord, my heart cries out for you in the day time, and my nights are restless for I long to be in your embrace, to feel your love rushing through me, to hear you say I love you. I long to hear your voice in the night, Lord! There is no beauty in me but you. You are my beauty, and your presence causes me to glow with brightness. Lord, make me beautiful to you always. Romance is a lie. Love is a vain emotion, but your love is real. Evermore give me this love. Lord, you cause me to rejoice in the morning.

You, Former Mercies

Dear Lord, where is your presence so dear and sweet? Where is the one for whom my heart beats? Where is the love that so abound? How can I know that you are around? Lord, I had been astray, looking for other things and going other ways. Lord, forgive me soon for my heart is full of gloom. My soul longs to feel your embrace; my heart longs to see you face-to-face. My body cries for you—for only you—and your love is true! Lord, let me, I pray, feel your breath upon me. I need you, Lord, today. How can I ever live without you? I can't, no way.

Father, I am so sorry for all the deceit I let rule me. You have been ever merciful to me, but one thing I ask is that you not remove your presence from me. Your anointing is so sweet. Lord, cause these bones that have been wounded to heal. Father God, I love you with all my heart, and I pray you will forgive my straying heart and bring me back to your ways.

(Written on Feb. 1, 2007, at 12:42 p.m. after realizing deceit in my heart)

Loving Arms

True story.

I was in a congregation for about three years, and I noticed that everyone who came after me was pairing off with someone and getting married. I was devastated. Was I that undesirable? How sad. Anyway, there was a wedding, and we served wine, and I drank some and we danced. But when I got home, I started crying. I was so lonely because I had no one to hold me. So the next day, at work, this man driving a truck took notice of me and blew his horn every time he saw me. Anyway, one day, he got the nerve, approached me (I have been told even by female friends that I look unapproachable), and gave me his number. We talked on the phone for a good eight months because every time we were supposed to go out, something happened.

Finally we went out for a date, and he took me to a place that sold catfish, and he ordered oysters. The next thing I knew, we were at some park, and he was trying to seduce me. He bought me four long-stem roses and put some secular love music on. He did not succeed, so he asked me if he could come to my house. I said no. This lasted for about two weeks; he wore me down with his persistence (I was working two jobs: one was for the school district and other was for security. I worked from 7:30 a.m. to 3:00 p.m. and from 3:30 p.m. to 11:30 p.m. respectively). So he was wearing down. One night, he called and asked, and I said, "Yes, but swear to me as a 'man of God' that you will not force me." He said OK. He arrived at my place around 12:00 a.m. He held me. One thing was leading to another, and the whole time, I was asking God to help me. Well, he got to third base, thinking he was going to hit a home run, but I reminded him of his promise, and he stopped trying. I had to sleep next to this man; God did not allow him to defile me. I learned from that, and I never let a man in my home again.

So I missed being held. Two years have passed from that time, and not too long ago, I had this desire just to praise God with all my heart. I was at a religious camp with my congregation (Beth Shalom, Dor Segulah), and I could not wait to just praise God. This was where I found my rest. From that point on, he has not ceased from holding me because he knows my every need. His arms are so big and tender, and he draws you into his arms of love to show you what's in a ketubah. He shows you what's under the chuppah. And when he brings you into his tents, you know his banner over you is true love. O Lord, your love has captivated me. O Lord, your love has brought me to my knees for eternal delights. O Lord, how lovely are your tents. O Lord, how lovely are your tents for eternal delights. I thank you for your love, Lord.

Why the Attacks

When growing up, I was introduced to waves of perversion. Things at home were not very wholesome either, so you can imagine that after my mother's death, I started really acting out of all I knew. HaSatan (Satan) is aware of that. He is also aware that Jesus redeemed my life from sexual perversion.

Since the Lord showed me that he loves me in a special way, I have been under attacks in my mind and thought process. It has now become a fight to keep impure thoughts out of my mind. After all, years ago—eleven years exactly—God cast out the spirit of perversion and that thing that kept me bound to cigarettes. That old snake, he always comes to steal, kill, and destroy the work the Lord is doing. I know I am free from the past, and so are you! If you are reminded of something you did years ago, know that the devil is a liar and a deceiver who tries to stop servants of the Most Highest God from proclaiming his name. He is love personified. He is the author of love, and I know he loves me.

He Loves You Too

I just want to share this for anyone who may be fighting past events that keep coming to mind. It is a lie. Whom the Son sets free is free indeed. I am free, and so are you. Jesus loves you! This is a true account of my life as it is now. I pray that the Lord will help anyone going through troubles or pain by me sharing the things God has done for me. He can do anything. Don't give up. Be like the widow with the unjust judge.

You Are My Shield and Buckler

As we sit here, waiting for the bell to ring to be dismissed, I look at the students, not understanding the strange sense of authority coming from me. I love to be social and very funny, yet I have felt as if you were not with me. And so I prayed that you would quiet them and keep them in subjection to me, and you did. It is very hard with some of them, but even with the difficulty, you have submitted them unto me. Thank you for answering my prayers, Lord. By this I do know you will never leave me again.

The Tire That Needed to Be Replaced

I just want to thank you, Lord, for your provision. I am aware that I cannot place you in a box. Yesterday—Wednesday, 15, 2007—I called my Firestone card to see if I had enough to get an oil change (I live paycheck to paycheck being a government employee). Anyway, I checked and found I had $40.00, so I said good. I was waiting for the car, and they came and told me I also needed a tire. That would altogether be about $60.00. "Ninety-two dollars and forty cents," the man called to find my balance, and all of a sudden I had $94.00 on the card. God, you are awesome and my only provider. Thank you for using what is meant for evil and providing for your children.

Dear Lord

What was it that happened to me? Why did I feel the need to change on the surface? I lost everything with high hopes of gain. My life is now hidden in Christ, the one who set me free. So now I can rejoice also with the redeemed. I no longer choose my way, but the Messiah in me all the way is not doing my own thing to see the dawning of a new day. He is the king. There is no one like him.

I will walk in the shadow of your wings, and in your presence I will sing. A new creation you have made me. Now you have lifted my head above all my adversaries. Oh, you are mighty in all your ways. Yes, in all your ways. Of your waters I drink freely, your wine gladdens me, your oil anoints me, and your love assures me.

You!

More than all, I need you more than words can say. The Lord of Glory, shine your light this way. Cause me to hear laughter in the morning and be held in your arms at night for, to you, I will give my heart and all my might. When evil surrounds me, I will pray. I will sing out loud each and every day. When I am forgotten, you've taken me in. For to you, I will seek to the very end. Open my eyes so I can see.

Let Me Hear Your Voice

Lord, let me hear your voice. Speak to me, my father. Let the words of comfort and edification spring from your lips to your servant. Let me, I pray, drink from your pool of wisdom that I may serve you completely with awe. Your wisdom is as pure as a newborn with its mother and as enduring as a father and his first-born son. Let your strength and beauty cover me. Let the your beauty cover me. Jesus, you are beautiful. I love you, Lord. Teach me to prove and show you my love.

Love Is More than Just Feelings

As I sit here thinking why I love thee, it is not based on what I hear or what I see. It is not due to what is done, but it is due to the one begotten Son—Jesus, savior, redeemer, and friend who submitted to the father to the end and who gave his life so passionately to save a broken sinner like me and to loosen and set me free so that I may follow him passionately. To die to self and live for Christ is one way I can sacrifice.

Thank you, Lord, for allowing me to be a partaker of your sufferings.

Love of My Life

The Lord is good and greatly to be praised. He is a shield and buckler to those who take hold of him. I love you, Lord, for you are at my right hand; and those who know you love me. I know there's nothing good but you. We, who are your children and made in your image, are to love one another as you have loved us.

Lord, you are my God, and I love you. You have shown me true love, and it is good. Lord, I think about you in the morning, and my body desires you all day.

O Lord, my flesh cries out for you. I long to dwell in your presence.

Lord, you are my lover and the husband of my youth. My desire for you will never cease.

Love like this should be outlawed for it is better than life. No man on earth can ever love me the way you do, and that is the reason I long to be with you. Made in your likeness, female, the presence in which it is pleasurable to dwell—all is pure, holy, and delightful. As long as I live, I will seek to drink from the river of life all the days of my life for in the rivers are pleasures forever more.

More Like You

Lord, I thank you for your great mercy and your awesome grace. You have been ever mindful of my weaknesses; you have not dealt me my just deserts even though you have allowed tests to come. You have not rewarded me the evil due to me.

You are more righteous than what words can say. Father, I ask that you would help me be more like your Son, Yeshua, Jesus. He was silent before his accusers, he was merciful to sinners, and he was a healer to the sick. He was gracious to the undeserving. Lord, help me be a blessing. When they strike me, give me strength to take it. If they need, make me able to give. Let your oil pour out of me like a lubricant for dry souls. Let living waters spring up in me that those who thirst may come and drink freely.

Lord, your word tells us to buy at all cost but to give freely. As you fill my cup, Lord, I will give freely to anyone who is in need. Let me, I pray, be a fountain full of living waters.

A Song in the Night

I will bless the Lord with all that is in me. I will praise his holy name. He who opens doors and no one shuts and shuts doors no one opens even has opened to me. I will tell of your goodness all day long. You are the God who gives wisdom and glory and gives strength to your people.

Who is like unto you, God, for heaven is your palace and the earth beneath you is your footstool? Who shall not fear you? You did wonders in Egypt and signs in the desert.

You gushed out water in dry land. You gave meat in the wilderness.

Who is a god like our God? Wonderful you are.

You gave us a king, David, to sit on the throne of your Father. What a mighty king we serve. He is the lion from the tribe of Judah, and he is our God. Holiness is his garment, and righteousness his crown. He is the Lord of Glory, and his name is Yeshua.

Oftentimes I find myself in constant battle between wanting to do right and wanting my vindication to be swift, but woe to the one who is quick to anger for he will surely suffer the wrath of God. How can I wish harm on those who do me wrong when I want the grace and mercy of God to abound to me when I trespass his righteous judgments? He truly is the rock in which I can do all things.

He Who Forgives

O holy one who forgives insolence and pride, the one who pardons proud speech, I thank you for not having consumed me in the fire of your displeasure. Only your mercy has sustained me. I have spoken evil against you, yet you have not held that charge against me. God of Abraham, Isaac, and Israel, forgive me for I had forgotten you and your power to execute judgment as you please. Lord, wipe the arrogance out of my heart and make me new again.

My Prayer for This Day

Lord, I long for your embrace. You are my source of life. With you there are living waters springing up into the well of life. You are my one true desire, and I need you for nothing in this world is more precious to me than you. Longing to be your treasured possession and washed by your blood. You have made me holy; no one else could. I live to be in your presence all day long. I want to fill your ears with loving songs. May you rejoice over me as in days of old so that I may walk in your ways completely bold. My heart is crying out for you, and nothing else in this world will do.

Lord, You Are Still with Me

Lord, you are faithful, and you will always confirm the weary. You have strengthened my heart with godly counsel. You have put gladness into my heart at a time I thought surely you have abandoned me.

Today, Feb. 2, 2007, for the third time, I was thinking about how I was a big flake, and surely you had removed from me your mantle. But then you comforted my weak heart with answered prayers from a week ago. Thank you for your faithfulness even when my heart wickedly doubts your care for me.

Be Still

I have been quieted by your presence and want your presence to dwell in me, and I abide it. To be *Echad* (one) with you O God is pure delight. All my flesh yearns for your breath upon me.

God, the Giver

Today is a good day full of expectation of his glory. May the Lord fill and use me to his pleasure for in him there is no lack. He is the provider of all things. He gives to men who are worthy a gift for a man who finds a wife finds a good thing and has obtained favor of the Lord. Likewise, the man who is scorned by the Lord will obtain a seductress who causes him to go astray like a wild beast of the field, and he will never find peace for the woman who is from God is the keeper of peace in the home. Shalom Beit for the man who has obtained favor of the Lord. He is the provider of that which is good. May you, Lord, shine your face on us today that we may reflect your glory.

Giving Thanks in the Morning to You

His is the glory, honor, and power. He is the strong tower. I will awake in the morning with a grateful heart and a singing spirit for a good start. Today is a day of praise. Let us rejoice in the Lord always. Lord, I love you with a sure heart. Let nothing and no one tear us apart. I have set my heart on praising you. I will never again lose my confidence in you. You are higher than the heavens, and I will enter into your presence. Thank you for a wonderful day, and let my life reflect your love today.

Spring Up

Awaken my soul to the Lord in the morning and let my song be of your wonder. In the early hours, I will seek your favor; and in the day, I will bless your name. You have not forgotten the cry of the weary for you are their shield. You will not allow the sun to strike by day or the fear to arise at night. You are a faithful Father who cares for your children. Lord, I love you with a pure love and thank you for your spirit. Oh, you fill me and my cup to overflow and let the river flow. You told the woman at the well, "If you drink the water I will give you, it will well up in you a spring of living waters" (or something like this in John 4, I believe). Let those rivers flow through me now with intensity. Let your spirit send forth its rain. Rain down on all who thirst for you. You are the fountain of living waters, and let me drink continually from your spring. Gold does not move me, silver does not attract me, but a day in your courts is what I long for. Let the new wine come and fill my heart with gladness, and I will sing your praise.

Time in His Word

A time of refreshing has come my way. Hours in his word I shall stay. He is like water to my soul. Through his spirit, I become bold. For in him, there are riches untold. So in him, I will cast my cares and empty my load. How wonderful are your rivers, and how magnificent is your grace. Call upon the Lord all who are hungry, and he will feed you with the bread of life! Blessed be the name of the Lord forever and ever.

Twenty-four Hours a Day

The Lord is a strong tower that set watch over our souls. The Lord unties the bondage, which keeps us in chains. And in his right hand, there is freedom; in his left hand, victory. He is a faithful God who does not turn away the cry of the afflicted. Cry to him all who are thirsty, and he shall fill your cup. In the midnight hour, stand before him for in him is shalom. He is the Sabbath Rest, and he is full of grace. Take time to seek the Lord in the dark of the night, and he will answer. He is willing to hear the shout of the oppressed.

In praising him, there is victory. All who hunger and thirst for righteousness shall be filled. Lord, teach us to drink from you the fountain of living waters, and we shall sing your praise.

Path to Freedom

Let go of anger, release bitterness, and confess before God your sins when all seems lost and deaf ears are around. He's listening. If someone has something against you, forgive them.

Declarations

I will love you, Lord my God, with fervent desire. I have set my heart to receive your fire. In the midnight hour, I will seek your power. In the daylight, I will walk in your might. In the afternoon, you will hear my voice. In the evening, I will pray. Lord, you are my one desire all my days. To know you more and more is what I live for. Thank you for placing in me the destiny you have for me—to become a daughter of the Most High God! You are to be praised, and in you, I am free.

Only in You

Your taste is sweet to my lips. Your fragrance around me is like incense. You make my heart leap for joy. In you is all my delight! Only in you is pure light shining, ever shining, shining so bright. You are able to save the sinful soul, and you make my body whole, wanting to be in your presence. Touched by the blood of the lamb, I enter to worship you only. As you heal my land, only in you is pure delight. You're holy, holy, holy, holy, and bright. You are able to save the sinful soul, and you make my body whole.

Love Covers a Multitude of Sin

I have never really understood this phrase until now. It is something learned, and I know how. I have to learn how to forgive. I have to learn how to let go. I not only have to learn how to walk, but I also have to learn how to talk. Lord, you taught me through your life; you never condemned the sinner or those looking for mercy. You never hated children. In fact you said, "For such is the kingdom of God." You welcomed children, and they were not to be turned away. Children will work nerves, but what else is love for. What is sin? Isn't it missing the mark? We've all done that, so no one has a right to judge another. The Lord did not even stone the woman found in adultery for he was the only one sin free. He covered her and loved her; and when everyone else tried to condemn her, he sent her away with these words, "Sin no more." His grace and goodness set that woman free. I can imagine how it must have been to look in the eyes of this loving, graceful man, such tenderness in his eyes. This is just one instance, but what about the woman who put oil on his head and washed his feet with her hair? She must have known how much he cared. A woman so full of sin yet has had it all lifted and loves more even to the end. This kind of love, I know, for sinful Chant'e had all the sin stripped away by her daddy.

Abba is his name, and I will never sin like that again for he covered all that mess, and now I'll do the same. Lord, as long as I live, your unfailing love to others I will give. Christ in me is the hope of glory!

Living Waters

Make me a fountain of living waters so my thirst will be quenched, springing up in me life eternal. Let those thirsty drink freely of the living waters flowing from me. Oh, my cause in life is to see the sick healed, the dead raised, and the Messiah revealed. Let my life be a walking epistle of your faithfulness. Let those I come in contact with leave me blessed! It is a hard life to live, I know, but nothing gladdens me more than light through me shone. It is a hard thing to do when you think to yourself, "Everyone must think I'm a fool." A doormat is what it feels like sometimes, but it is all of a process of believing called dying to see lives change, and out of a drought comes rain—falling, falling down, not to the knees or ankles, but enough water to drown. Send the clouds with water ready, and let the showers come nice and heavy. Let it wash over me, and may it send an incredible release. Let blind eyes open, deaf ears hear, down arms rise, and limp feet dance with cheer. Let it come as a mighty wave just as the earth shook before they lay Yeshua in the grave. The same and more we will do, so let this latter rain spew from you.

Lord, you are our source, and this is no lie. So under the shadow of your wings, let me die. You know what that means, Yeshua, my Lord, my lover, and my everything. Oh yes, your name is awesome, and you are glorious, my king of kings and my eternal rest. One so holy, how can this be that your holiness would ever listen to me? I am just dust before the wind, yet you have called me friend.

Dear Diary II

The more I know of you, the more I want to know you. You are my strength and shield. Lord, to you my soul cries out; and through the Holy Spirit, I yield to do those things hard to do like to offer my life as a living sacrifice for you, to bless those who curse me, to pray, and to set them free. Lord, help me be a vessel pleasing to you so I can offer my best to you—not like Cain who slew his brother but like Rachel's favorite son, Jacob, the other. Let my desire go before you until the day I am to wed someone given to me from you. Let my children be delightful in your sight, and let me someday become a wonderful bride to a son who has won your favor by entering into your rest from his labor.

You Heard Me

Truly the Lord is my salvation. He has avenged me of my adversary for no reason at all. Wicked words of hate are thrown toward me, but the Lord was my stronghold when I cried out to him night and day. Lord, you heard me. You told me to worship you and to praise you. And through many tears, a sacrifice of praise was offered to you. You heard me from your loftiest heights, and now I shall reflect on your goodness all the days of my life. You are my only rock. Lord, teach me to number my days that I may walk free from offense. May my lips never offend anyone. Show me your ways that I might live. Show me where I am falling short, and I will turn from it. For surely you hate the deeds of the wicked, but you are ever merciful to those who seek you. Thank you for delivering me from those who hate me and rise up against me for no reason just to break me down and tear me to pieces with no one to help. But you heard my cry.

Through It All

Lord, I will sing to you for you have done marvelous things when my enemy rises up against me to tear me to piece. You will be my rock. I will trust you, Lord, for you are my deliverer. You will defend me from those too strong for me. I will dance before you, my king, with all my heart. Let my body bring you praise and the lifting of my hands bless your holy name. As I look only to you, be my guide for in the shadow of your wings I long to hide. I will stand and will not be moved for I know that your faithfulness you will prove. Thank you for loving me and showing me your mighty hand able to set me free.

My Cry

Sing to the Lord a new song. Make a joyful sound before his throne. Worship him in the morning. Bless his holy name at night. Come before his presence with tears of joy and fall at his feet.

He is holy, righteous, and worthy. Let my cry go before your ears this day and answer me. Let my soul rejoice in the God of my salvation and be covered as with a shield with your glory. Holiness is your mantle. Let it consume me.

Prayer of Confession and Healing

The Lord is my healer and my saving strength. He has become my fortress and shield. He has taken all my illnesses on his body that I might walk in healing. The Lord, Yeshua, has done all things well. He has made the blind see and the deaf hear. He is my manufactor; therefore I will trust in him.

You, Lord, have made me whole by your blood. Thank you, Lord, for your healing power. Thank you for setting the captives free. Thank you for listening and hearing me. Bow down your ear to my cry for it is not from profane lips.

Father, I beseech you. Heal me according to your truth in your word. You have come that I may have life and that more abundantly. In the name of Yeshua, I am healed.

This Morning

I set my face like flint to do your will, to walk in love and cause trembling to be still. Fear is not the result of one who believes, but through him, I have been relieved. My thoughts focused and my motives true, Lord, to honor, to walk, and to serve you. May you increase and I decrease so your power can rise up in me. You are my source of life, and I need you even in my waking hour. If I cry, you answer me with thick clouds. You've come to my rescue. Oh, you are my king and can do anything. Yeshua, you are holy and wonderful, and your train fills this temple. When will I be satisfied? Only when I awaken in your likeness.

May my actions reflect yours and my words speak life. May the voice of singing be heard in the morning and the lifting up of the hands as incense. If I were to tell of your wonder, I would faint for I would never go anywhere. I would be writing for hours and hours and hours of your goodness and grace. You have loved me yet in sin, and you never cast me out even when I turned my back on you. You stood there with open arms like a mother waiting to receive a wayward son. So you waited for me to return to you, my love, my blameless king. You bore the sins of the world on your back, and I am sure my sin was a heavy weight. Thank you, Lord, for loving me while I was still in sin and accepting me back into the sheepfold.

Gracious

The Lord is truly gracious, merciful, and true. He has not allowed me to suffer great loss, just a few. His word is written in my heart, which I think is a good start. All other things can be replaced; this is God's grace. My car was there, and so was my bass. My expensive things are hard to replace, but God had me calm all the way. And now I thank him for yet another day. I wish I could tell you I will be glad to have the thief found, but I was not really mad. The Lord gives and takes away, and even if he didn't, he knew about it yesterday. I was so relaxed till I saw the other security driving two young girls around the parking structure of the mall. They knew not where their car was at all, and my heart bled for them. Their car was stolen, not just broken in.

I was able to pray with them. The police saw it all and wondered about my Jewish New Testament. So this was a time for the Lord to shine in my time of need; he's not mine. To witness his care for others and not just mine and the girls with me to witness the peace in the storm, his glory is divine. This gave God glory and not caused me harm. He has already told me he is going to pay for my window fixing; I don't have to worry at all about a thing. I just praise him like I do, and he will see me through. Going back, my first love is an adventurous ups and downs to see if my heart is pure. I pray he sees me through. Lord, let my life reflect you.

Vengeance

The Lord is my defender, and he is my shield. To him I owe my life. He is the restorer of the sick and the helper of the helpless. In him I do trust. My soul cries out for the living God and longs for his vengeance upon those who rise up against me for no reason. For no reason at all, they tear at me with their lips, speaking vile things. Lord, in your truth, vindicate me. Let your hand not be kind to any wicked persecutor. Let your judgment come as a thief in the night on those who hate me for no cause. You are my God and king. I have given up my life to see your power working in others, and they have become prideful and have caused me to run in anguish—lying one to another and speaking proudly as they tear me to pieces with evil thoughts. Lord, send forth your wrath upon them suddenly so they will not see the sun nor the light of day. I wish I had wings, and I would fly far away, but I cannot—I must stay. But, Lord, my heart has been broken. But you are near to the brokenhearted, and you hear their cry. Lord, cause my righteous cause to spring up before those who hate. Let the young rise up and take the land since the aged refuse to enter and prevent others from entering it. Lord, let us rise and cause the enemy to run seven ways as we boldly proclaim we are the generation to possess the land.

Thought for Today

What if I want something that's not meant for me?

I sometimes think I may want something that God knows may not be the best thing for me. What if I want to marry, but he wants me to stay free? What if I want to have children, but he wants me to be a mother type for children whose parents are not quite right? Will I love them less because they are not from my womb? Woe is me. Why do I think like this daily? I have grown up way before my time, and now I sound like I am about eighty years old. What if God actually wants me to enjoy life because worrying won't change a thing? What if I am to be happy, but because of confusion, I believe I am sad? What if?

What if, on the other hand, he wants me to live a life of suffering and reproach? Can I do it?

On the other hand, Yeshua (Jesus) came so that we might have life more abundantly. On the other hand, he also says that we would suffer persecution and to pick up our cross and follow him. On the other hand, there is always another hand. Until he returns and the full mystery has been unveiled, I will seek him with all my heart till I awake in his likeness.

High School Basketball

OK, besides being a security guard and crossing guard, I am also a "campus supervisor" at Arlington High School in Riverside. Anyhow, today was the game against J. W. North High—an exciting matchup indeed. I went to support my guys and took my dad with me. The games were very exciting. Freshmen lost though, but they played a good game. Next the JV came in and dominated the game. Lastly, the varsity; this was indeed a good game. Arlington Lions were ahead most of the game. The game ended up in double overtime. Did I say double? I meant triple, and we lost by two, 78 to 76. Both teams were excellent, but the parents sitting on the side I was on were horrible. The things they said about the players and the things they yelled to their players to do to Arlington players were terrible. The foulness of language and the violence in the heart over a high school basketball game are incredible. As the first overtime minutes were being played, I heard someone say, "Fifteen is hurt," gloating over the fact that an opponent was injured. I sat in disbelief as the children were copying the adult's action. One of the north players elbowed someone in the face. What are people teaching their children? These were grown men and women yelling and using vulgar language at the officials. Yes, I know some of the calls were bad for both teams, but to swear and threaten is totally out of order.

I never really understood the point of team sports until tonight. It is amazing where God will speak to you if you want to hear from him.

I don't, but if I did, I hope I would not have that kind of murder in my heart over a high school basketball game or any sport. You know, Yeshua (a.k.a. Jesus) said, "If you hate your brother without a cause, it is the same as murdering him." According to Jesus, a lot of murderers are walking around daily.

On the last game, I went to an Arlington parent who was talking foolishly about another player of Corona High, and I corrected her after the game.

She apologized. We must learn to be graceful when things do not go our way instead of being hateful. I am not a prayer about games or sports because those who have the better skill should win, but I do pray that the young men on both teams will not learn to do what the adults did because that would be sin.

May the Lord forgive all those hateful and angry parents. I wanted to yell at the parents, not the players. The parents were wrong.

I just had to get this off my chest. God bless!

A Little Different

I am a little different as you can see, but the strange way I live my life makes me, me.

I love to confuse people about what to expect for they don't know what I will do next. I look a certain way, and actions should follow. I believe in a better today, not a good tomorrow for what if tomorrow never comes? Then I would be totally bummed.

Only You

More than all I want to know is you. More than words can say, I love you, Lord, more and more each day. My heart, soul, and flesh cry out to feel your embrace. Only to see you face-to-face. Moment by moment brings thoughts anew, only to be closer to you. All my bones desire your touch for only your touch is ever enough. Lord, I love you with all my heart. Let my life speak of my relationship with you forever.

Restore Me Again

To you I pray, lifting up my heart, hoping to please you with my life. I have strayed from your arms, having hopes of a family of my own. I have let my thoughts go astray; please forgive me. You are the lover of my soul;

why should I hope for anything else? Maybe it is not wrong to think about a husband and children; but I feel, in some ways, I have left my first love. Can you ever forgive me, Lord? Let your love satisfy me in the night and keep me during the day.

Thanks and Praise

You have been more gracious to me than I could ever hope for. All my life, I have never known what I was missing. You have been my saving strength in every weakening hour. I love you, Lord. Thank you for your mercy.

The Heart of the Redeemed

The Lord is high and lifted up, and his ways are beyond knowing; his thoughts, unsearchable.

The one who forgives and heals is his name. I will suffer with him for he has suffered for me. I will bear the sins of many for he has borne my many sins. His name is Yeshua, savior.

I had forgotten his kindness; that's why I was not kind. I had not remembered him overlooking my offenses; that's why I was offended. O Lord, you are the lover of my soul; and for you, I will suffer. I will take what you allow me to have; and when it gets too heavy, I will call out to you, my God, and you shall answer me. You shall answer me with a voice of thunder, and you will roar like a lion to deliver me from the jaws of my enemies.

The Lord Is My Life

Love, I will make mention of you in the morning and will sing to you in the evening.

You are my life. In you, I have placed all my hope. I love you, Lord, for you have first loved me. You make my soul desire your love. O Lord, you are good, and those who know you know you are good. And your taste is like honey. I wish my arms could grab hold of you; I would never let you go. You are my eternal delight, and I will sing your praise. Lord, thank you for your Shekinah (glory) residing in my heart. It is my constant desire.

Wonder

You put the stars in the sky. You made the fish swarm in the sea. You formed man from dust and gave him dominion over the works of your hands so he can represent you on earth. You took woman from his side to help him feel alive; to work with him and be a coair; and to love, hold, and have children to bear. Thank you that you love us so much for it is you I long to touch. You are holy, righteous, and true. Let my heart, which cries out, reach you.

Thank You

Worship the Lord in the beauty of holiness. Fall down before his throne and open your mouth with shouts of praise. Leap before him for he is worthy. O peoples of the earth, love the Lord with all your heart, soul, and mind for he is waiting to bless you! Let your heart rejoice and your being take pleasure in the lover of your soul. He is the husband of the widow and the lover of the lonely. He is the father of the fatherless and the provider of the needy. So call on him in times of trouble and remember him in times of plenty for he is always longing for the whole hearts of his people. God of Israel, I love you. Let your spirit fill me to overflow for in you there is no lack. What else is there to say!

A Better Sacrifice

May my actions speak out loud to you. And my words, let them be few. Let my walk be a rosebud sending up sweet fragrance to you. Let the lifting of my hands be as the morning sacrifice even though you paid the ultimate price. To the cross you were led, spikes in your hands and a crown of thorns on your head. Hanging for hours at a time, suddenly you gave up the ghost. You never died, descending into hell and conquering death so that we may enter into your rest, freely given without price—unlike the red heifer—but a better sacrifice.

In You Alone

I will sing to you, Lord, for you are great and greatly to be praised. You have given me more than I can imagine. You are my saving grace. In you alone is my destiny. In you alone is my victory. I walk in your ways all my days. You are my victory. Hell and death could not keep you, strong and mighty God, defending the weak and weary from the power of the dog. You are my salvation; in you I wait all day long. To you I cry out at night, and in the morning, I'll sing my praise song. In you is my destiny. In you is my victory! I'll walk in your ways all my days. You are my victory!

Hopeful

Israel is a place I have not thought of for a while, but I am in need of some serious warfare. When I was younger, I did nothing but seek God, and his power was at work in me mightily. He healed the sick, cast out spirits, and brought peace. He corrected, and he also used me to execute judgment. I want that back. I thought of nothing else but him. What happened? I don't know, but I do know that thinking about other things have distracted me, and now I am all but helpless. The kingdom of God is not in words but in power. Let this be true in my life again.

My Plea

Lord, you are awesome, and I just want to say that.

I feel like praising you, and I want you to receive my praise as liquid incense before your throne.

Let my voice excite you in the morning and draw you at night. And let the scent of roses be on my lips. If I could create the best songs, I would. If I could hold the longest note, I would. If I did not crack or go off-key, if I knew how to play professionally, and if I could build you a house or dance a thousand hours a day, I would. The only problem is that I can't earn something freely given; your love was free to me because you created me. You are my manufacturer. If I am broken, you can fix me, so I confess I need fixing. But you are so worthy, Lord.

Let this broken heart rejoice before you again as in times passed where nothing shook me. Where did that go? So fill me once again to overflow. Lord, you know how to help the helpless. I hope you will not be weary of me bugging you everyday until those words I long to hear you say.

Do You Want to Get Married?

What a question to ask. I guess this is a personal blog and should be in my diary, but I have nothing to hide and nothing to be ashamed of. Do I want to get married? Of course I do, but to whom? Wherever I go, there is no one for me, so I will live my life content while I am free. Maybe I should go out and fix myself up, but will that really be enough? Would I be willing to do that daily? Not really. I like to be comfortable; sweats and tennis shoes are what I want to do. Can I be accepted as I am living to please God, not looking for a man? I want one, yes indeed, but only if that is a part of my destiny. I long to be held in the arms of my own, to have a house ready when he comes home, and to raise children in with fear of the Lord. What else is there to live for? I want to be considered beautiful but always cute and never anymore—never fitting in with the crowd and never showing my pain of rejection out loud. Marriage after marriage, I have been wondering. Lord, will that ever be me, going home day after day, trying to ignore the hurt away? But still, in all, I know that the Lord is gracious. Knowing the beginning from the end and having been born for such a time as this walking in power, in that I am blessed. God knows what is best for me; so he let me be unattractive, even ugly, in some people's opinion. And that is fine; it has helped me keep God on my mind. To know he has not rejected me is good enough, and maybe I will be pleasing to him in my life. If I can reign and rule with him in the end, it will have been worth it. So I hope this clears things up for those who have asked, and maybe God will be pleased with me at last.

Will You?

Learning to let go and trusting God is easy for me, but trusting him through people is hard. You see I've learned that most people are full of it. You know that word; they just act in front of you. But when not around you they talk and make fun of you. I never believed I could let go with people because I have been let down, but God now wants to turn that around. I am a part of his body, and we need each other—fathers, mothers, sisters, and brothers. If I fall, will you catch me? or will I drown? This is why I trusted no one at all. I have had very little encouragement from older people because some of them pray for my defeat, but God is on my side. This I know, so I have no need to hide. I thank the Lord for this learning process so that I may offer him my best.

I Can't Sleep

I can't sleep; what else is new? So I took this time to write to you. My heart is calm, and my thoughts are sure. Everything I do toward you is pure. To praise you is my strength, and to worship you is my pleasure. I'll delight in you forever. Cover me with your wings. I want to know you. In your presence, I long to stay. A need stronger than that of food and a desire more intense than fire, let me burn. Drown me in your river of love. Thank you, Lord! In you is a gentle touch; that's why I love you so much. I want more of you each day, to know you more and more. Soaking in your presence is all I want. Let me be drawn into you. O Lord, I long for your touch every night; the washing waves flow through me from the crown of my head to my feet. What a release!

Point of No Return

I know you're looking for someone strong, one to whom your heart belongs. You're looking for a wife so true, one who would never turn her back on you and one who goes forward with your work and doesn't let her mind go berserk. My Lord, I was on the verge of turning, but you kept my heart yearning. Looking back to the past was going to be my downfall at last. But then you reminded me from that vomit; you set me free. Should I be like a dog because I wallowed like a hog? Thank you for your light so pure and for my choice not to wander far but to stay near. Thank you for all that you do, so I may obey you, not out of fear or fright but because I know it is right. Thank you once again, and now I know I will fight to the end.

Remember

God, I thank you for your many blessings.

I love your ways, and I love that you can trust me. You are my eternal hope. I want you to know I love you. You are the reason I sing. Thank you for those you have put in my life. I hope my life will encourage them to be all they can be in you. I pray you are pleased with me. Forgive me for this slow response to your request for truly you are worthy of double honor, Lord.

I pray your blessings will flow, and you will be lifted up for your goodness. And yet when we struggle, I pray a sacrifice of praise will be seen in our lives. Let my actions speak louder than any words, and let me be a blessing to you and my fellow servants. You are worthy, Lord. Be glorified!

Part 3

SONGS OF THE LORD

God of Israel

Lyrics and music by Chant'e Holsey

My thoughts shall be of your strength
You have been my meditation
To you, I will render praise
I will prostrate myself before you

Chorus

You are the God of Israel
You are the God of Israel

Stretching forth your hands to heal me
Wash me from all my sins
Came once as a suffering servant
As a king, you'll come again

You are the God of Israel
You are the God of Israel

You are the way, the truth, and the light
A pure and holy sacrifice
The spotless lamb who paid the price
To you, I owe my life

Only in You

Your taste is sweet to my lips
Your fragrance around me as incense
You make my heart leap for joy
In you is all my delight
Only in you is pure light
Shining, ever shining, shining so bright
You are able to save the sinful soul
And you make my body whole

Wanting to be in your presence
Touched by the blood of the lamb
Enter to worship you only
As you heal my land
Only in you is pure delight
You're holy, holy, holy, holy, and bright
You are able to save the sinful soul
And you make my body whole

O Lord, I Glorify Your Name

Lyrics and music by Chant'e Holsey
Intro Chords: A, C, D, E

O Lord, our Lord, how excellent is thy name in all the earth
O Lord, our Lord, how excellent is thy name in all the earth

Out of the mouth of babes and suckling thy has ordained strength
To still the hand of the enemy and to silence the avenger
To bind up their kings with chains and their nobles with feathers of iron
To execute vengeance of the heathen and judgment upon the people
O Lord, our Lord, how excellent is thy name in all the earth

I glorify your name
I glorify your name
I glorify your name
I glorify your name

Yeshua
Yeshua
Yeshua
Yeshua

El Shaddai Adonai, Elohai, Yeshua
El Shaddai Adonai, Elohai, Yeshua
El Shaddai Adonai, Elohai, Yeshua
El Shaddai Adonai, Elohai, Yeshua

Holy, Holy, Holy
Holy, Holy, Holy
Holy, Holy, Holy
Holy, Holy, Holy

I praise you, my King
I praise you, my King
I praise you, my Lord
I praise you, my Lord

Hallelujah
Hallelujah
Hallelujah
Hallelujah

Let the Jealousy (Your Name Is)

Lyrics and music by Chant'e Holsey
Intro Chords: C, G, A, F, C, G, F twice

Let the jealousy of your love fall on me
Keep me as the apple of your eye
Create in me a pure heart
That I may show forth your praise

Let the jealousy of your love fall on me
Keep me as the apple of your eye
Create in me a pure heart
That I may show forth your praise

Show forth your praise
Show forth your praise

Your name is above every name (Yeshua)
Your name is above every name (Yeshua)
Your name is above every name (Yeshua)
Your name is above every name

Let the jealousy of your love fall on me
Keep me as the apple of your eye
Create in me a pure heart
That I may show forth your praise

Show forth your praise
Show forth your praise

Let the fire of your love consume me
Let the fire of your love consume me
Let the fire of your love consume me
Let the fire of your love consume me

And I will praise you for you are worthy of all glory
And I will praise you for you are worthy of all glory
And I will praise you for you are worthy of all glory
And I will praise you for you are worthy of all glory

The Lord, My God (Yeshua)

Lyrics and words by Chant'e Holsey

I will sing and I'll dance
I will glory in romance
Of the Lord, my God, Yeshua
I will jump and I'll shout
To the one who called me out
To the Lord, my God, Yeshua

For he is my portion
Almighty friend is he
He has destroyed all of my enemies

Redeemed

by Chant'e Holsey

Lia, lia, lialialialialialia, lialia, lia, lialia, lia
Lia, lia, lialialialialialia, lialia, lia, lialia, lia

Glory to the lamb of God
Who died for me on Calvary

Who died and was buried and rose again
Who died and was buried and rose again
Who redeemed my life from destruction
Who redeemed my life from destruction

God of Vengeance

by Chant'e Holsey

Lialialialia
God on vengeance show thyself

Lord of the whole earth, shall the throne of iniquity prevail? Gathered against the righteous, innocent blood is shed, you are the strong rock of your people Israel

The Lord God, merciful and gracious. Long suffering, abundant in goodness, and truth. Keeping mercy for thousands, forgiving iniquity and sin. You are the strong rock of your people Israel

Lialialia

To the God of Israel

To the God of Israel, the holy one who never fails, blessed is he who formed the heavens and the earth. Who teaches my hands to war and my heart to praise. Living to make my life so free till in your image I am made.

Final Thoughts

I like to thank God, my redeemer—Yeshua, the Moshiach, Jesus, the Christ—for his unfailing love and acceptance. He is the God of Israel and the God of all creation. Six days he made the earth and everything in it, and the seventh day he rested and was refreshed. He is the bright and morning star and the lion and the lamb. His name alone is to be lifted up and praised. All authority was given to him, and for him and by him was all things created. In him dwells the fullness of the Godhead in bodily form—the perfect image of the invisible God.

Blessed be your name, Lord Jesus (Yeshua) forever and ever. Selah!

Contact Information

I would like to hear any comments you may have. Please send any remarks to PO Box 2772 Riverside, California 92516, or you may e-mail me at shirelle3too1@yahoo.com.

May the Lord give the reader *wisdom and* understanding. *May God bless you and fill your heart with Holy fire!!!*

In Messiah's service,
Chant'e Holsey a.k.a. Ashirah Azriela

About the Author

I am Ashirah Azriela a.k.a. Chant'e Shirelle Holsey.

I was born to Ralph and Eva Holsey on May 25, 1974, in Dominquez Valley Hospital. There I was given the name Chant'e Shirelle Holsey by one of the nurses. She said of me, "She looks like a Chant'e Shirelle," and my dad called me Chant'e Shirelle. The name Chant'e is French for *singer* or *sung*.

From the time I can remember, I was taught the word of God; and at the age of five, I went to the altar by myself and was baptized in the name of Jesus. This was the beginning of my walk with the God of Abraham, Isaac, and Jacob.

Growing up in a black family in America was hard enough where the ministry of self-hatred and embarrassment was prevalent. All this I learned from the aged around me, but in the midst of all this, the Lord was speaking to me.

As early as seven years of age, I can remember praying that God would make me like King David, a person after his own heart. The next thing I remember is my mother reading from the Old Testament and saying to myself, "This is for me." After that, I remember watching a movie called *King of Kings* and saying to myself, "I am going to Israel because I want to walk where Jesus walked and the stones are pretty." Next I remember my fascination with Jewish people and how they were chosen by God. I soon started looking up the names of the tribes to find where I fit as a child.

This is a writing of who I am in the Lord and how he has brought me to this *point* in my life. In this book, you will find a short biography, prayers, writings, songs, and psalms, which the Lord has given to me. I pray that *God will touch the hearts of all who read this work and fill them with a holy fire.* Lord, let your spirit minister to the readers of this book.

www.ingramcontent.com/pod-product-compliance
Lightning Source LLC
Chambersburg PA
CBHW050012070726
47598CB00014B/737

* 9 7 8 1 9 5 4 6 7 3 5 5 7 *